COMMIT

HOW TO BLAST THROUGH PROBLEMS & REACH
YOUR GOALS THROUGH MASSIVE ACTION

LINDA FORMICHELLI

CONTENTS

1

WHAT IS COMMITTING AND WHY THE HECK DO I CARE?

*W*e humans have a big problem: We have exciting goals and dreams, but we feel stuck. We spend a lot of time thinking about the actions we need to take, but don't actually do them consistently. We then become overwhelmed with our day-to-day lives and let our dreams languish...and we settle for lives of mediocrity and regret.

Or, we have problems that keep us from being our best selves, but don't have the energy or know-how to defeat them. Money woes. Relationship issues. Health problems. And more.

And sometimes, we experience both situations: Dying dreams and too many problems.

Can you relate?

Thinking small—living inside the box, keeping our greatness inside us—is what consigns us to this life of what-ifs and if-onlys. If we have *big* dreams and *big* problems, we need to go after them in a *big* way. That's what *Commit* is all about.

A COMMIT STORY.

*F*or four months in 2008, I woke up early every morning in a state of sheer panic. My heart beat like a jackhammer, and my stomach rebelled with waves of nausea. This hell lasted from when I got up until four or five in the afternoon. Every. Single. Day. On top of this was clinical depression that made it difficult for me to get out of bed, and impossible to work.

While I'd had panic disorder for 20 years and had half-heartedly tried various methods to quell the panic over the decades, I found this situation completely unbearable, and threw every tactic I could think of at the problem, all at the same time. Meditation, yoga, various medications, talk therapy, light therapy, aromatherapy, life coaching, acupuncture, homeopathy, Rescue Remedy—you name it, I did it.

Until, on May 2, 2008...the panic disappeared and never came back. For someone with a long history of panic disorder, this was obviously a life-changer.

Which method did the trick? I'll never know. It may have been just one of the tactics I tried, or it may have been a combination of two or more. But I don't feel I wasted my time or money on the ones that didn't work, because just knowing I was taking multiple massive actions to heal every day made me feel more in control during this rough time.

I haven't had a panic attack since that day. And when I feel anxiety building, I have a whole arsenal of approaches I've become adept at from that period. I try one after the other until the anxiety dissolves. Usually, it takes just one or two methods from my extensive bag of tricks.

This is what I call Committing: Overwhelming your problem or blasting toward your goal using every ounce of energy, resources, and knowledge you have.

A COMMIT FAIL.

*N*ow, let me tell you about a time I failed to Commit, and the consequences.

In 2007, my husband and I rescued two cats from the shelter. Misha was 9 and Sasha was 11. Over the next seven years, these cats destroyed, bit by bit, two sofa sets and a beautiful rug.

When we noticed the damage they were causing, we tried putting SoftPaws on the cats. For those of you who aren't familiar, SoftPaws are little plastic caps you literally superglue over each of your cat's claws, which is a time consuming and annoying process for both the cat and its owner.

The SoftPaws slowed the destruction somewhat, but even with the caps on the cats could still damage the furniture—and when one of the caps fell off, as they do when a cat sheds its claws, the cat was able to use that single claw to wreak untold devastation. It was kind of amazing, really.

We tried several kinds of cat scratchers, from the sisal ones you hang from a doorknob to the corrugated cardboard type that lies on the floor. Misha and Sasha looked at these scratchers with expressions that said, "You're kidding, right?" Every once in awhile we would rub the scratchers with catnip, and the cats would become intensely interested in them until the scent wore off a day or so later.

Then we bought an herbal cat repellant, which repelled the cats for approximately five minutes.

Finally, I covered the corners of the sofas with double-sided tape. The cats were irritated when the tape stuck to their paws, but they persevered and eventually the tape would come loose. Every week or two I would have to re-tape the furniture.

You know how the problem finally resolved itself? In 2014, both cats died of old age.

For seven years we tried one tactic after another to save our possessions, to no avail. But what if we had Committed to solving the problem? We would have fitted the cats with Soft-Paws, taped the corners of the sofas, sprayed the furniture with cat repellant, bought a *big* scratching post—one of the fancy ones with different levels and toys attached—and rubbed it with catnip every single day. We would have done this all at once instead of trying one tactic at a time.

I have a feeling that if we had truly Committed to solving the issue, we would have saved the load of money we spent on replacing our furniture and rug.

COMMIT TO WIN.

ommitting is *taking massive action to solve a problem or reach a goal.* It's pretty much the opposite of the baby-steps approach. When you Commit, you do whatever it takes to make happen what you want to happen. You can use one giant, crazy, unbelievably powerful tactic, but it's even more effective to combine several tactics at the same time—which we'll talk about later.

Committing is also about gathering so many resources and so much support that you simply can't go wrong. Later, we'll talk about hiring help, creating accountability, and buying (or borrowing) the right supplies to get off to a mighty start.

WHY COMMITTING WORKS.

*Y*ou've probably noticed that when you start a project or a new adventure, or set a new goal, you're extra motivated at first. *Commit* is about concentrating and harnessing that initial motivation to such a degree that it propels you right past any roadblocks you may run into later.

There are four major ways Committing works for you:

1. It gives you explosively fast results.

When you take the baby-steps approach of chipping away at a problem or goal a little at a time, the results you want are a long way off. This causes you to become disappointed and disillusioned, and to give up before you reach your goal.

When you Commit, chances are you'll see results very quickly. For example, say you want to lose 10 pounds. You read one of those ubiquitous articles on how to shed weight by making small changes, and decide to cut out your daily can of Coke. Doing this, you'll save 140 calories a day, which means you'll lose one pound every 25 days. It will take you about eight months to lose those 10 extra pounds. But you get discouraged and give up well before then.

Now, if you *Commit* to losing the weight, you'll spend an hour tossing out all the processed and junk foods in your pantry. You'll buy or borrow ten cookbooks that feature light, healthy recipes, read through them all, pick out a month's worth of meals, and stock your pantry and fridge with all the ingredients you'll need to make them. Then you'll join a website that helps people find fitness buddies, and sign on with a local buddy to walk, run, or pump iron together several mornings per week.

Notice that these Commit tactics are cheap or free. If you have some cash to spare, you'll also visit a nutritionist who can help you develop a meal plan, and hire a personal trainer to come to your house three mornings a week to give you a tough circuit-training workout.

You can't do all that and *not* see quick results.

2. It boosts your motivation.

It's easy to lose your spark when a goal seems far off in the distance, you're taking teeny tiny steps to get there—and you're not seeing discernible results.

Faster results mean more motivation for you. If you're trying to save money, for example, and you see your bank account growing quickly thanks to your massive action, you'll be more inspired to stick with it.

As another example, my Renegade Writer Press co-publisher and good friend Diana Burrell wrote a diet book where she interviewed people who had lost weight and kept it off. She was surprised by how many had embarked on their journeys by getting sick, such as with the flu, which jump-started their weight loss. Losing five to ten pounds that way made them not want to gain it back, so they began to eat healthfully and continued shedding pounds. (I'm not saying you want to get sick to lose weight, but that fast results equals more motivation!)

3. It automates your goals.

Once you get the Commit ball rolling with massive action up front, it will keep going on its own, without much extra effort from you.

For example, if you take the massive actions we talked about above to lose weight, all the pieces will remain in place unless you actively stop them. The fitness buddy will come by three times per week, you'll have an arsenal of light recipes on hand, and your pantry will remain clear of tempting junk food (unless you go to the effort of restocking it with cheddar-horseradish chips and Nutrageous bars). The process is automated, so it gets easier and easier.

4. It makes you feel good.

Even if you *don't* see results right away, Committing to solve a problem or reach a goal helps you feel in control, boosts your self-esteem, and overall makes you feel better about your life and yourself. You're taking control, and it feels good!

This is what I experienced when I was going through those four horrific months of daily panic attacks. I couldn't control the panic at first, but I *could* control my reaction and what I did about it. That helped me get through a very tough time.

There are a lot of things you can't control—when you will get hired, how much you'll earn as a solopreneur, when you'll connect with that someone special, when you'll feel better—but there are a lot of things you *can* control.

In my Commit fail with the cats the consequences were pretty minor, but on the big stage that is your life, failing to

Commit to your goals (and to solve your problems) can lead to struggle, regret, mediocrity, and failure. You'll be left wondering why you never succeeded in business, why you were never able to lose that weight, why you never shared your art with the world, why you settled for negative relationships—in short, why you got to the end of your life with your fire smoldering inside you.

My philosophy is that we're here on earth for just a short while, so we don't have time to mess around with half-hearted attempts and false starts. If you want to be extraordinary and do extraordinary things, you have to do it *now*—and do it big.

In upcoming sections, we're going to talk about how to get ready to start Committing; how to Commit by reading a massive amount of material, hiring help, embracing discomfort, putting some skin in the game, and more; how to put together your Commit plan; and how to troubleshoot the obstacles that are getting in the way of your Committing.

WHERE COMMITTING WORKS.

*C*ommitting works with so many areas of your life it's kind of ridiculous. For example:

Business: Starting a business, finding new clients, earning more income, creating work/life balance, getting publicity.

Health: Preventing disease, solving chronic health issues, going vegetarian/vegan/paleo, building muscle, losing weight, training for an athletic challenge.

Career: Finding a job, changing careers, getting a promotion, going after a raise, doing better work at work.

Finances: Getting out of a financial hole, paying down debt, saving money, earning more.

Art: Creating more, selling more, boosting your creativity, getting your art seen.

Emotional/mental issues: Overcoming anxiety, depression, ADD. (Yes, there is the caveat that you may need professional help! Hiring help is one of the Commit tactics we'll talk about later.)

Relationships: Making new friends, finding a romantic partner, solving relationship problems, handling parenting issues.

Later, I'll outline some of the tactics you can choose from to tackle any of these challenges or problems with overwhelming force, as well as how to combine the tactics to create your own personal Commit plan.

COMMIT'S ORIGIN STORY.

a while back, I read a blog post on using what the author called "overwhelming force" to solve your problems. I enjoyed the post and filed it away in the back of my mind.

Then, a few years later, I did a review of my past and realized that every time my life moved forward in an amazing way, it was because I had Committed by using this philosophy of over-whelming force—that is, by taking some huge actions. For example:

- When I was starting out as a freelance writer, I churned out dozens and dozens of magazine article queries, letters of introduction, and sales letters— nonstop. My first year in business, I beat out the income from my former office job by 50%. Within two years, I was writing for top magazines and businesses.
- I beat panic for good by throwing every solution I could think of at the problem, all at once. (It's been almost 10 years since then and I've been 100% panic attack free!)

- To save money so I could make a full-time living working part-time, we moved from New Hampshire to North Carolina, within two months of making the decision—which helped us save over $20,000 per year.
- When I wanted to cut down my work hours even more to homeschool our son, I crammed my feed reader with blogs about saving money and made a huge dent in our monthly expenditures—enough to cover much of the loss of income I experienced when I went down to working just a few hours per week.

As I reviewed how Committing changed my life in such incredible ways, I thought, "This is something I need to share with the world!"

As someone who used to mentor and teach writers, I've seen many, many aspiring scribes give up on their dreams before they even gave them a chance. (How many people want to be writers, and how many people are actually doing it?) And writers aren't the least of it: All kinds of people resign themselves to living lives they don't love because they simply don't know how to Commit themselves to solving their problems and reaching their goals.

My methods, I realized, could be condensed down to their essence to help people change their lives. So I researched the most impactful ways to get off to a powerful start—a start that increases motivation to untold levels and propels people past their blocks—and *Commit* was born.

Now...are you ready to start Committing to reaching your goals? Keep reading for details on how to prepare, why you should stop complaining already, and 20 ways to Commit.

2

GETTING READY TO COMMIT

I can feel the excitement: You're ready to get started Committing! But hold on there, friend—first we need to spend just a few minutes preparing and going over some important details, so you can get off to an explosive start.

THE ONE MAJOR PIECE OF EQUIPMENT
YOU NEED RIGHT NOW.

*T*he major piece of equipment you'll need to start Committing is...drum roll...a notebook. (Oh yeah, and a pen would be nice, too.)

That's right: You don't need a computer, expensive software, or the hottest new app. You just need some paper and a pen to write down the goal you want to reach or the problem you want to solve; your *Commit NOW!* assignments (more on that below); your ideas; and your results.

You *could* open a word processing document on your laptop, or use an online journaling program, or type notes into your phone...and that would be fine. But there's something about a physical notebook that you can carry around and flip open no matter where you are that makes Committing easier, more satisfying, and more fun.

So my advice is to spend ten bucks on a nice-looking lined notebook that you would enjoy writing in, plus a high-quality pen.

CHOOSING A GOAL OR PROBLEM TO COMMIT TO.

*O*nce you have your notebook and pen ready, take some time to consider what goal or problem you'd like to Commit to first.

When you've become experienced at Committing, you may be able to Commit to multiple goals at once. But for now, choose just one. We want to get you off to the most powerful start possible, and it's difficult to do that when your attentions are divided among several problems or goals. So let's just experiment with one thing to start with.

Having trouble figuring out which of your many goals or problems to Commit to? You could simply select the biggest, hairiest one—the problem that keeps you up nights, or the goal that's been burning in your soul for months.

Or, conversely, you can brainstorm a huge list of all your problems and goals, and try to knock off the one you feel would be the easiest to tackle. This will help you rack up an easy "win" and build the momentum to go after your bigger goals. For example, save for later the goal to get your art into galleries, find the love of your life, or be able to stop taking your meds for Type

2 diabetes. Instead, select the more manageable goal to lose 10 pounds, declutter your home, or improve your website traffic.

But you don't want it to be *too* easy. Your subconscious will rebel at Committing all your resources to a goal or problem that just isn't that important or exciting to you.

Keep writing...once you have the right goal or problem, you'll feel it. Your gut will tell you when you've found the perfect thing to Commit to right now.

YOUR COMMIT NOW! ASSIGNMENTS.

a s you read, hold in your mind the one problem you'd like to solve or goal you want to reach. At the end of each section, you'll find a *Commit NOW!* assignment you can work on immediately to bring you closer to your problem resolution or goal.

There are 20 tactics here, and I'd like you to choose the ones that resonate with you—or pick one *big*, audacious one—and start implementing them immediately. Remember, though, that combining Commit methods can help you get off to an even faster, better start. (More on that later.)

STOP YOUR KVETCHING.

I once posted a cartoon on Facebook where a patient said to her doctor, "I don't feel well, and I don't know why." The doctor replied, "Start exercising, meditate daily, eat more organic fruits and vegetables, get rid of your TV, try not to stress about things you can't control, and come back and see me in three weeks."

One lady went crazy over this. "Sure, maybe this will work if you have only one kid (*zing!*), but not for people with *heavy responsibilities*," she wrote. This suburban dweller of what was voted one of the "happiest cities in America" went on to rant that inner-city residents don't have access to organic fruits and vegetables, and that people who aren't feeling well need "tangible relief"—which I take to mean quick-fix medications that mask the symptoms—not lifestyle advice.

Then there was the writer in a writers' forum who insisted that all the advice the resident experts were offering was no good because it didn't apply to her very specific situation of being stalked by an ex and needing to keep her identity private online.

Look: I realize that not 100% of this advice will work for 100% of people. But that doesn't make the advice any less valid.

I can't account for every life situation or eventuality, but I can guarantee that somehow, there is a way for you, no matter what your situation, to take massive action to solve your problems or reach your goals. Your ways of Committing may be completely different from my ways, or your neighbor's, or your best friend's —and that's okay.

When people complain that they simply *can't do* something that would be good for them or make them happier, it's usually a BS excuse. We all have choices. The choices may not be ideal, and you may not like them, but they are choices nonetheless. So when someone tells me they can't, say, spend the time and money to get healthy, what I hear is merely that the options for doing so are unpalatable. If they have cable TV and two hours a day to watch it, they have the time and money to get healthy.

Or, even if the time and money thing is the dead truth, they still have options. They may have to swap childcare with a local parent to free up time to exercise, give up some expenditures in order to hire a trainer, learn to grow their own organic fruits and vegetables, take a healthy cooking class, or go to a marriage counselor to solve the problem of why their spouse will never, ever watch the kids for a measly 15 minutes so they can meditate. These are all tough choices and take some effort to set up...and for many people, maintaining the status quo is so much easier and more comfortable.

Please don't confuse "This makes me uncomfortable" with "This is impossible."

Don't dig around for reasons something *won't* work for you —think about ways you *can* make it work. I'm not saying it will be easy or comfortable, but that's not the point. Change can be hard—at least at first, until it becomes habit. But if you can just muster up the resolve to get through some up-front discomfort, you can reap the benefits of massive action. We'll be talking more about this discomfort soon.

Below, I have 20 ideas on how to truly Commit to defeating your problems or blasting off to your goals. This isn't a list of every possible Commit tactic in the universe—not by a long shot. These ideas are just to get you started, and once you get into the Commit groove, you'll probably discover other methods that work for you as well. Later, I'll also tell you about Commit's secret weapon: Combining tactics to get off to an even mightier start.

Now, let's Commit!

3

UP YOUR MENTAL GAME

a lot of Committing is about changing your mind. And I don't mean waffling between whether to have the chicken or the fish at your favorite restaurant—I mean developing a Commit mindset that will help you reach your goal or solve your problem. From thinking ridiculously big to letting go of lesser goals, in this chapter we'll talk about Committing from the inside out.

COMMIT TACTIC #1: EMBRACE DISCOMFORT.

*R*ecently I was talking with a friend who tends to experience periods of very low energy. I told him, "Cold showers have been shown to help with that...or at least, turning the temperature to cold for the last couple minutes of your shower, which is what I do when I feel sluggish."

"God," he shuddered. "That sounds so *uncomfortable!*"

If you're not at least a little uncomfortable, you're probably not Committing.

I listed this Commit tactic first because it's the one that will affect every other method you try. Change—whether it's negative or mind-blowingly positive—is always uncomfortable. When you disrupt well-worn habits, even if they're bad habits, your mind will resist at first. Going all-in to solve a problem or reach a goal means you'll be stretching yourself in new ways, and that can make you feel stressed, annoyed, or even fearful. For example:

- If you want to lose weight, eschewing your favorite processed snacks might make you annoyed and cranky at first.

- When you want to become an author or an artist, showing your creations to other people can stress you out.
- If you're looking to simplify, it may be unsettling to get rid of items you've been hanging onto forever.
- You know public speaking can help you get the word out about your consulting business, but it's so scary!
- If you want to improve your relationship with your spouse, saying "I love you" every day when you're not used to doing it will feel uncomfortable and weird at first.

Instead of avoiding discomfort, embrace it, knowing that it means you're stretching, growing—and Committing. The good news is that while change is uncomfortable, the discomfort is temporary: It lasts only until you've established your new habit and started seeing benefits. And since Committing is designed to build motivation quickly and get fast results, the amount of time you're feeling stressed, angry, or fearful is likely to be short.

However, I hate self-help books that give advice like "Embrace discomfort." I always think, "Yeah, I'll get right on that." The big question is, *how* can you do this challenging, nebulous thing?

Here are some ideas to help you make it through those first few minutes, days, or weeks of discomfort as you start to Commit to your goal:

- **Talk to someone who's been there.** In all likelihood, that person will tell you they were uncomfortable at first, but after a while they started feeling more confident, less stressed, etc. For example, if you ask almost any successful writer how they felt when they were getting started, they'll tell you they were scared out of their wits and every cell in their brain was screaming for them to choose a safer career. It's not just you, and you can move past it just like they did!

- **Meditate.** Daily meditation—just sitting and focusing on the breath—can help you come to grips with your feelings of discomfort. If, like me, you need help with meditating and the whole focus-on-the-breath thing doesn't cut it for you, I recommend the free guided meditation podcasts at The Meditation Podcast (www.meditationpodcast.com). My favorite is the "Positive Thoughts" meditation, which has you visualize success in various areas of your life. Another option is the mega-popular Headspace app (www.headspace.com), which offers guided meditation series to tackle anxiety, help you become more productive, and more.

- **Give yourself a pep talk.** Affirmations are positive statements you write down and read to yourself several times per day, and some people find them effective for building confidence. For example, an affirmation for someone who wants to get a promotion at work may be, "I'm the best person for this new position at work, and the quality of my customer service proves it to my bosses every day. Even though I feel fear that I might not get the promotion or that, if I do get it, I might be in over my head, I'm working right through that fear and am moving forward with confidence and joy."

- **Suck it up.** In her book *Feel the Fear and Do It Anyway*, Susan Jeffers points out that people who succeed at great things aren't unafraid; they're as uncomfortable as you are when they try something new, but they just feel the discomfort and move forward in spite of it. This is an option for anyone in *any* situation! Realize that you *will* feel fear, annoyance, stress, and so on—and Commit to doing what it takes to reach your goals even as the negative feelings are present in your body and mind.

Commit NOW! In your Commit journal, write down some of the ways you predict going after your goal will make you uncomfortable. Then, come up with a plan for dealing with the negative feelings that will arise. Will you give yourself a pep talk? Call a friend to talk it out? Meditate? Suck it up and move on?

COMMIT TACTIC #2: CLEAR THE DECKS.

*T*his is a good place to tell you why I didn't Commit to marketing this book. I Committed to *writing* it, but not to actually *selling* it—even though my goal is to spread the word about *Commit* as far as I can.

As you'll read throughout *Commit*, I have devoted myself to being at my computer as little as possible. After years of hustling as a freelance writer, I decided I wanted to have more time to take care of home and family. By using several Commit tactics, including moving to another state, I finally made this plan a reality.

Then this book came along. I spoke with a business coach who discussed with me all the money and effort that goes into a proper book launch. As I listened, my stomach sank. As much as I wanted to get this book into the hands of as many people as possible, I simply did not want to have to start (another) blog, run contests, and contact hundreds of personal development bloggers to beg them for a mention.

Later, I chatted with my life coach Kristin Taliaferro and she pointed out that when you Commit to a goal, other goals will necessarily fall by the wayside. For example, if you're 100% Committed to training for an Ironman triathlon, you probably won't be also Committing to launching a business, writing your memoir, or learning a new skill. And you have to be okay with that.

Also: Often, you can't easily Commit to two things at once because the goals conflict with one another. You're Committing to losing 50 pounds, and you also have a goal of starting a cupcake store? Conflict. Want to work more and relax more? Conflict.

The same with me: My goals of working as little as possible and orchestrating a huge book launch were like oil and water. Dogs and cats. Tyson and Holyfield. You get the idea.

So when you launch your Commit practice, know that other aspects of your life may get short shrift, at least temporarily. You might need to cut down on socializing, order take-out dinners or get someone else to cook, set aside your vacation plans, hire someone else to manage your business, or reset your expectations for how clean your house is.

If you have two Commitments that conflict on the surface, you may be able to brainstorm ways to make both goals work within your new parameters. Maybe you *can* lose 50 pounds while opening a cupcake store, if you get a partner to do the baking and tasting. Maybe you *can* work more and relax more, if you hire someone to do your chores and run your errands. This is where you'll want to think creatively.

Commit NOW! In your Commit notebook, list the aspects of your life you may need to let go of to fully do your Commit practice, and come up with ways to mitigate anything you feel is unacceptable. For example, if you simply can't let your house go while you launch your business, can you delegate cleaning to the kids or hire a housecleaner?

If your Commit goal conflicts with another important goal, brainstorm ways to make them both work. Rope in a friend to help you, if you can—other people can often spot opportunities that are not apparent to you.

COMMIT TACTIC #3: MAKE IT NON-OPTIONAL.

*M*any people don't reach their goals because those goals are not based on life-or-death motivations. The world won't end if you don't start that business. You won't die if you don't learn Spanish, declutter the house, or repair the rift with your spouse. If you don't finish your dissertation, you'll be disappointed but you won't be in any actual danger. There's always later, so why stress about it now?

But what would you do if you *had* to reach your goal —or else?

This is a trick I learned when I trained to be a wellness coach: I would ask clients, "If your doctor told you that you had to lose those 30 pounds in four months or you would die, what would you do to lose the weight in a healthful way?"

My clients would brainstorm and come up with ideas that they never would have thought of without that motivation. They might consider hiring a personal chef who's trained in healthy cooking, going to a weight-loss camp, doing the Whole30 challenge (more on that later in this book), or completing a doctor-assisted weight-loss program. These may sound extreme, but hello!—death is knocking on your door! You are highly motivated, to say the least.

Seems expensive, right? I recently had an experience that demonstrates how going all-out in this way can sometimes be cheaper than the alternative. I'd been feeling unwell and kept wishing I could visit an integrative physician, since my regular doctor couldn't figure out the problem...but it was so expensive I kept putting it off. Then I ended up in the emergency room. The emergency docs couldn't uncover the cause of my illness either, and I was hit with a $5,000 bill. I learned my lesson and made an appointment with that integrative doc, who did a load of testing and discovered, among other things, that I'm intolerant to whey. (How sad for someone whose favorite food group is dairy!) The cost? $2,000. Wish I had done that in the first place.

This "life-or-death" thought experiment helps you figure out your options, keeps you from playing it too safe, and helps you Commit to your goal with a burning sense of purpose. For example:

- Imagine that if you don't raise $10,000 for your favorite non-profit by next June, they'll have to shut their doors and will leave dozens of poverty-stricken families homeless. What can you do?
- An eccentric billionaire offers you a million dollars if you learn to figure skate in two months. What would you do?
- A big New York publisher tells you that if you get together enough short stories for a collection in three weeks, they'll publish it, pay you a huge advance, and get the book into bookstores. How would you get those stories done on time?
- You may not have the time to meditate now, but I'll bet you'll somehow find the time if your doctor lets

you know that you're on the brink of a total nervous collapse.

- Your garage is stuffed to the gills, but you win a $4.5-million Lamborghini Veneno that must be sheltered from the elements, and it arrives in five days. How can you get that garage cleaned out ASAP?

Commit NOW! Grab your notebook! Whatever your goal or situation is, dream up a scenario where you *must* get it done, and then brainstorm ways to make it happen. Then: Start putting your new, larger-than-life plan into action right now.

COMMIT TACTIC #4: CONNECT YOUR
GOAL TO A LARGER PURPOSE.

*Y*our goal is to overhaul your diet. The reason? Your doctor told you it will help lower your blood sugar levels. And yet, whenever you're faced with a choice of what to nosh on, your brain resists the baby carrots and sends you racing straight to the giant bag of M&Ms.

In wellness coaching, we're taught to help clients figure out the higher purpose behind their goals—a purpose so important and right that it makes them truly want to work until they realize their dream. If you're working for the right reason, nothing will keep you from reaching your goals.

For some of us, looking great and feeling confident in our clothes are the weight-loss motivations that resonate the most. For others of us, it's that we want to be around to see our grand-kids get married.

If you want to ace your college classes, your higher purpose might be to land a high-paying job after graduation...it might be to use your knowledge to help others...or it might be to gain self-confidence so you can move through life with a sense of ease. There are no right or wrong answers here.

Figuring out the purpose that will drive you to Commit is

not easy. If it were, you would already know what it is and you wouldn't be reading this book. It takes some soul searching to know *why you want to do what you want to do.*

I've been there. For years, I set the annual goal to earn a certain amount of income. But then I wouldn't actually, you know, change the way I worked, and at the end of the year I'd wonder why I once again had missed the mark.

Finally, I figured out that I don't care about the exact amount of money I make. What I care about is earning enough income to feel free: Free to do what I want, free to not have to stress about paying the bills, free to fulfill my other life goals without worrying about how I can afford it. Freedom is a feeling, not a number.

So your higher purpose for your goal—the one that will make you want to truly Commit—might be to provide you with emotions and experiences like:

- Love
- Freedom
- Security
- Giving
- Confidence
- Loving how you look
- Happiness
- Providing for others
- Leaving a legacy
- Helping others reach their own goals
- Making the world a better place

Your mind isn't stupid, and it has an amazing B.S. detector. If you want it to Commit, you'd better give it a darn good reason.

Commit NOW! Grab your Commit notebook and journal about why you want to do what you want to do. You'll know when you have the right reason: You'll be hit with a feeling of inspiration and motivation. (And don't worry—if you start out with a particular "why" behind your goals and it ends up not resonating with you, you can always choose a new one. It's all an experiment!)

COMMIT TACTIC #5: GO BIG OR GO HOME.

*H*ave you ever felt just plain *stuck* every time you contemplate how to reach a long-held goal? You keep coming up with the same ideas you've already decided wouldn't work, and your motivation plummets.

Maybe it's because you're limiting yourself by playing it too safe.

Here's something to think about that will help you break out of this trap: What's the *one* thing you can do that would demolish your problem or blast you toward your goal—no matter how crazy, expensive, or impossible that action might seem? Forget *reason*, ditch *practical*, and strike the word *impossible* from your vocabulary.

Sometimes, just pinpointing the very best, no-fail action and stating it aloud (or writing it down), even if it's a nutty-sounding, giant, audacious idea, can help propel you in the right direction.

For example, several years ago my goal was to work fewer than 20 hours per week, but still earn a full-time income. I streamlined my work habits and chipped away at our expenses, but it dawned on me that the reason it was hard to make this plan work was that living in New England was just so freaking expensive.

The big, crazy idea I had? As I mentioned in Chapter One, it was to move somewhere cheaper.

Two months later, my family and I were living in North Carolina. We saved $400 per month on mortgage alone. My parents, who had moved to North Carolina a few years earlier, cared for our toddler during our work hours, which saved us $600 every month in childcare. Our health insurance dropped from $750 per month to just over $200. And just think about how much we save on heat in the winter! (Our heating bill exceeded $500 per month in snowy New Hampshire.)

Now, I know not everyone wants to move across the country or shake up their lives in a huge way, but *you need to explore all your options*. For example:

- If you're unhappy at work, maybe you can quit your job and do something completely different.
- To solve a societal problem, you could start a nonprofit.
- You're burned out on the daily grind: You could pull the kids out of school for a year, travel the country, and homeschool on the road.
- If you have no time to train for a marathon, one possibility is to get up at 3 am to run.
- Sick of living paycheck to paycheck? Building a $100,000 cash cushion is one possible goal.

Again, you don't have to actually *do* any of these things. (Though you certainly can. Regular people like you and me start nonprofits every day...I read about a dad who took his son couch-surfing and skateboarding in all 50 states in one year. And the internet is full of blogs written by people who quit their snooze-worthy jobs and are now working for themselves from some tropical island.)

The real goal of dreaming this big is to get you thinking outside the lines. For example, maybe you can't pull your kids out of school and travel the country, but that crazy idea might spur the more manageable idea to plan day trips every weekend for the next six months. As another example, the idea of quitting your job and changing careers might be a no-go, but maybe you *can* look into other positions within your current company that are more along the lines of what you want to do.

And maybe, just maybe, you'll want to actually implement one of your mind-blowingly big ideas. Again, people do these things all the time, so in most cases your craziest idea is quite doable. Every day people pick up and move to new states, apply to medical schools, change careers, launch themselves on around-the-world journeys, and more.

Commit NOW! Make a list of the ten most outrageous ideas you can to reach your goal or solve your problem. Forget reason and practicality. Don't censor yourself...just write. Then seriously consider each idea. Could you actually do it? If not, does it bring up ideas for something you *could* do?

COMMIT TACTIC #6: CHECK IN WITH YOURSELF.

*E*ver have this happen to you? You're Committed to working toward your goal of climbing out of debt. You decide to start off today by negotiating down your insurance premiums, and you jump online to find your insurance company's phone number.

Then, three hours later, you wake up from a daze of Facebook, Instagram, and cat videos. What happened to the day? Well, there's always tomorrow.

And tomorrow. And tomorrow.

Don't worry, it happens to all of us. But luckily, I have a trick for shaking yourself out of the haze of distractions that consumes your day, so that you can focus on Committing.

The trick is to check in with yourself at predetermined intervals of time and ask yourself, "Is this what I want to be doing right now?"

Set your phone alarm to beep every 30 minutes (or 15 minutes, or hour—you choose!) so you can ask yourself this incisive question. Then you have the chance, over and over, to make a decision that will change the course of your day...and your life.

For example:

- *Beep!* You're aimlessly surfing the internet: Is this what I want to be doing right now, or would I rather be marketing my business?
- *Beep!* You're on the commute to work, listening to a morning shock jock: Is this what I want to be doing right now, or would listening to a podcast from an industry leader be a better use of my time?
- *Beep!* You're mindlessly snacking on Fritos: Is this what I want to be doing right now, or would I be better off doing a few pushups?
- *Beep!* You're watching an infomercial at 1 am: Is this what I want to be doing right now, or would I rather be creating art while I'm up all hours with insomnia?
- *Beep!* You're ruminating, with the same negative thoughts going around and around in your brain: Is this what I want to be doing right now, or would I rather be meditating or reading an uplifting book?

You'll likely be shocked when you discover how much of your day is frittered away on distractions that won't help you achieve your goals.

This sounds like a lot of phone beeping, but take heart that you don't have to do it forever. After a day or two, you'll become adept at waking yourself up from a stupor of busyness and distraction and staying on task toward your goals.

Commit NOW! Right now, set your watch or phone to go off at regular intervals so you can check in and ask yourself if what you're doing right now is what you really want to be doing.

COMMIT TACTIC #7: PUT SOME SKIN IN THE GAME.

A goal that doesn't involve risk is probably not a goal that will motivate you. A safe, bland goal will result in safe, bland actions. If you don't get your house decluttered, so what? You planned to go vegan but failed? No one cares. You didn't lose those last ten pounds...big whoop. In all these cases, you lose nothing.

But if you put some skin (money, effort, your reputation) in the game, it has to get done no matter what. After all, if you Commit like this and don't come through, you look like a fool. And no one wants to look like a fool.

Here's how to leverage risk as one of your Commit tactics:

- If you want to paint pet portraits for a living, run a "beautiful pet" contest: Pet owners send in photos of their kitty or pooch, and the winner gets a custom-painted portrait of their pet. Once the photos start rolling in, you'd better get your act together and figure out how you'll make it work.
- Say you've been putting off cleaning out your house, and it's gotten to the point that you can't walk across

a room without tripping over something. Pick a date in the near future for a yard sale, then buy a classified ad in the newspaper (or post on Craigslist, which is free). Bargain hunters *will* show up at your home at 6:30 am the day of your yard sale, whether you're ready or not.

- Make a pledge on Facebook that you're going to lose 30 pounds/go vegan/launch your business/write a book/clean out your garage by X date/stop eating out at restaurants to save money.

- Bet your best friend an amount of money that's painful but that won't make you go broke that you'll reach your Commit goal. For example, I bet a friend that I'd stop indulging in a certain time-waster, and if I failed I'd have to donate $1,000 to the reelection campaign of a politician I find particularly repugnant. That was three months ago as of this writing, and so far that $1,000 is still in my bank account.

In terms of putting skin in the game, creativity is more important than cash. Not all of these tips involve losing money —in fact, with the yard sale one, you'll *make* much more than the $15 you'll spend on a classified ad. If money is a sticking point for you, brainstorm ideas for putting something on the line that won't require cash.

Commit NOW! Open your Commit notebook and take notes on how you can put something on the line that will make it more likely that you'll Commit to solving your problem or reaching your goal. Take step one *right now*.

4

BY THE NUMBERS

*C*ommitting is all about doing lots of things, lots of times. Here, we'll talk about how to Commit by doubling your effort, moving faster, measuring your progress, reading piles of books and blogs, and other tactics that rely on sheer numbers to get things done.

COMMIT TACTIC #8: READ TEN (OR MORE) BOOKS ON THE SUBJECT.

*H*ere's how most people operate: They set a goal to, say, open a bakery. They buy a book on the topic, read half of it, and then let the book languish on their nightstand (and their dreams languish in their heads) as urgent-but-not-important tasks take over their days.

Instead, imagine racing through ten or more books on the topic of your goal. Some authorities claim that if you read ten books on any subject, you'll know more about that topic than most of the population. I agree. Quickly gaining expert status in the area of your goal will give you the know-how you need to make it happen.

Also, learning is motivational. I know that the more I learn about something, the more I want to actually do it. For example, when I wanted to learn how to better market my e-courses, a $19 SkillShare course and a virtual armful of marketing books got me all fired up to try out new techniques.

Yes, ten books is a lot of reading! But that's what Committing is all about: using overwhelming force to wrestle your problems into submission and blast off toward your goals.

How can you add this tactic to your Commit arsenal? Here

are some ways to Commit your way to success through reading a colossal amount of information:

- Maybe you want to build your nest egg: Find ten books on finances and saving money and read them, highlighting the sections that most resonate with you.
- You're having trouble disciplining your child: Gather ten books on parenting topics and take notes on the best discipline tips.
- You want to start a freelance web design business: Spend an hour researching the many, many books out there on the topic, pick ten, and read them all as quickly as you can.
- Looking to lose weight? Almost every bookstore has an entire section devoted to books for you. Rack up ten and you'll be able to create the perfect plan to shed pounds. (Not to mention you'll be inspired to do it—these books are highly motivational.)
- You're an aspiring painter, and you want to eventually show your work: Find ten books that will help you improve your technique and learn how to get your art into galleries. Read one. Repeat ten times.
- You're suffering from anxiety: Books on meditation, relaxation techniques, and how to beat stress and anxiety abound. Buy or borrow ten, read them.
- You wish you had a romantic partner, but you're too shy to approach people you're interested in: Gather up ten books on relationships, how to overcome shyness, and how to attract a mate. Read them all, and you'll soon have the knowledge and motivation to start connecting with new people.

To make this task easier, many people have helpfully compiled lists online of "Top 10 Books on Subject X." I just did a quick Google search and found a list of top ten advertising books, for example.

You don't have to spend a lot of money on this. We have this wonderful thing called a library that's full of books you can borrow gratis, and e-books are often inexpensive. But if you have the cash, nothing says Commit like an armload of beautiful new books from the bookstore.

If you buy physical books, instead of scattering them around your home or workspace, try keeping them in one big pile along with your Commit notebook and pen. Having a giant pile of books simply screams "Commit!"

Commit NOW! Search online for the ten books you want to read that will help you master your goal or solve your problem. If you have an e-reader such as a Kindle or Nook, or an e-reader app on your phone or tablet, you can get most of the books right away. Or, take your list to the library or bookstore and start building your stack. Then read your way through the pile, taking notes and highlighting passages you want to remember.

COMMIT TACTIC #9: OVERWHELM YOUR GOAL WITH SHEER NUMBERS.

*L*et's say your goal is to find that special someone to share your life with. Most people would let their nosy aunt set up the occasional blind date, and become discouraged as they go month after month without hearing the angels sing.

But what if, instead of going on dates every so often, you went to speed dating events where you meet a dozen potential mates for a few minutes each?

If you do something dozens, hundreds, or thousands of times, you almost *can't* fail. Peter Bowerman, author of *The Well-Fed Writer*, once said that you can strap an order form to a dog's back, and if he goes to enough doors he'll eventually make a sale. That's the kind of thing I'm talking about here.

For example, for The Renegade Writer blog I once interviewed a writer who e-mailed 300 trade magazine editors—and landed more than a dozen regular clients and over 80 requests for writing samples. That is basically enough to go from zero gigs to making a full-time living as a writer. That is a life changer!

The success you'll likely see if you hammer at your goal with a barrage of actions will boost your motivation, which will keep you moving with excitement and joy until you hit your target. In fact, even *before* you see success, the momentum of starting out super strong will push you through that initial resistance many of us feel when we start a new project. (Remember that discomfort we talked about earlier?)

To illustrate, let's try this thought experiment: Tell yourself, "I'm going to make three sales calls today." How does it feel? Most likely, it feels *meh*. Now, tell yourself, "I'm going to make 50 sales calls today." Which are you more excited to do?

Here are some more ideas for throwing giant numbers at your goal:

- If you want to raise money for breast cancer research by doing one of those 5k walks, instead of emailing a handful of friends to ask them to sponsor you, send a fundraising letter out to 250 friends, relatives, business associates, and local business owners.
- If you're an aspiring author, instead of sending your book query out to one or two agents, make a list of 75 agents that handle your type of book and send your query to all of them at once.
- If you're in sales, cold call 50 prospects per day.
- To declutter your messy home, vow to toss or donate 100 items in one day.
- You want to become a personal trainer and you have no clients. Send out the word that you're offering free half-hour sessions to 50 people. (I did this and ended up with two clients right away—and this was *before* I completed my certification.)

If you get creative, you can probably think up a way to throw big numbers at almost any goal. And even better, once you do *one* of something, it's not that hard to do it again. Write one fundraising letter and you can mail it out hundreds of times. The 50th cold call or training session will be much, much easier than the first. It would be a shame to expend all that effort doing something just one or two times when, with a little more effort, you could do it in multiples—and multiply your results as well.

Commit NOW! What can you do at least 50 times that will help you crush your problem or reach your target? Brainstorm ideas for using the overwhelming force of sheer numbers, and make plans to put at least one of them into action right now.

COMMIT TACTIC #10: MAKE A LIST OF 100 IDEAS.

*Y*ou could make a list of five ideas for mastering your goal or solving your pressing problem—and you'll probably dismiss every one of them as missing the mark. But make a list of 100 of *anything*, and at least one of your attempts is bound to be pure gold.

My Renegade Writer Press co-publisher Diana Burrell teaches an e-course called "Become an Idea Machine," and she has her students list tons and tons of article ideas. Yes, many of these ideas are worthless—but that's the point. Diana's students dump these ideas out of their heads and are surprised at the gems that turn up.

Another proponent of the big list is life coach Kristin Taliaferro. She suggests people write down a list of 100 "tolerations"—those little things that bug you, like "The dog keeps jumping on my bed" or "My nails are a mess" or "My refrigerator is too loud" or "My coworker keeps taking credit for my ideas." This is a way to take massive action to boost joy: Pinpoint *every single thing* that's annoying you and make a prioritized plan to eliminate each one.

In the same way, I recommend sitting down with your

Commit notebook and banging out 100 ideas on how to reach your goal or solve your problem. Don't judge the ideas or worry about which ones are best. Having to come up with 100 items helps clear the chaff from your mind so the great ideas can reveal themselves. At the same time, as you struggle to reach 100 items, your ideas will become more and more outrageous—which is a *good* thing, as we saw earlier in this book.

For example, you can list:

- 100 ideas for new ways to market your fledgling business
- 100 new ideas for homeschooling lessons and projects
- 100 ways to make more friends
- 100 ways to lose 10 pounds
- 100 ideas for saving your marriage
- 100 ways to add more creativity into your life
- 100 ways to get your kids to stop calling you at work

Somewhere in that great mind dump, you'll likely find a few ideas that will really do the job for you. The more you write, the crazier your ideas will get as you reach to fill the 100 slots. Those zany ideas might just be where the gold is.

Commit NOW! Grab your Commit notebook and blast out a list of 100 ideas for solving your problem or reaching your goal. Crazy, outsized ideas are not only okay—they're encouraged. Then, choose your best idea and start implementing it right away.

COMMIT TACTIC #11: DO A 30-DAY CHALLENGE.

*I*magine competing against like-minded compadres to reach a common goal, or competing against yourself with a no-excuses deadline in sight. Your competitive spirit is ignited, and you feed off the positive pressure as your goal gets closer and closer.

If you could use a push to Commit to your goal, try participating in a 30-day challenge—either a pre-arranged one, or a challenge you make up for yourself. For example:

- National Novel Writing Month (NaNoWriMo) is a competition where, according to their website (www.nanowrimo.org), "On November 1, participants begin working toward the goal of writing a 50,000-word novel by 11:59 PM on November 30." One writer I spoke with joined the competition and completed her first novel—at age 11. "Since then I've always known that I can do this writing thing, no matter what people say," she says. "And every year I write a new book, even if it's awful, because writing is what I do."

- The Whole30 Program (www.whole30.com) is a challenge to eat only whole, unprocessed foods for 30 days. The challenge has a paleo slant, and requires you to eliminate grains, sugar, dairy, and processed foods from your diet. Thousands of people have taken the Whole30 challenge to lose weight and get healthier.
- Some people create their own 30-day challenges; for example, they may challenge themselves to get up earlier, journal daily, cut out soda, spend less money, quit bad habits, and more. Just knowing the obligation is temporary helps it feel less overwhelming and increases motivation. You can set up your own 30-day challenge for just about anything.

These challenges allow for no slip-ups, no backtracking, and no excuses. In the Whole30 challenge, you can't "accidentally" eat a handful of your kid's Goldfish crackers. When you participate in a 30-day challenge to do 50 pushups per day, if you do 49 one Sunday because you're hung over, you lose. In NaNoWriMo, at the end of the challenge you either have a 50,000-word novel or you don't.

This is not meant to discourage you, but to steel your resolve. You are embarking on a challenge that's, well, challenging. Knowing it's temporary and that there's a goal in sight—in just 30 days—will help you squeeze out that final pushup, those last 50 words, the willpower to resist that cracker your son left on his plate. (We'll talk more about limiting your Commit time later in the book.)

Commit NOW! Whatever your problem or goal is, turn your

Commit practice into a 30-day challenge. You can find lots of challenges online that include accountability and camaraderie with other participants, or you can create your own. In your Commit journal, jot down what your challenge will be, and start today.

COMMIT TACTIC #12: FILL EVERY SPARE MOMENT.

*W*ork, school, family, church, volunteering...you're busy with a capital B. The everyday details of simply running your life crowd out your most important goals, leaving you feeling frustrated and resentful. Can you relate?

I have a friend who's a prodigious knitter. She's always turning out amazing hats, sweaters, and socks, even though she works and takes care of her family. Her secret? Wherever she goes, she carries her bag of knitting materials, so if she's cooling her heels in a waiting room or waiting for a show to start, she can get in a few stitches.

My friend is always approached by people—people who are sitting in waiting rooms with nothing in their hands, or staring off into space while they wait for the curtain to rise—who say, "If I had more time, I'd knit too" or "I wish *I* had time to knit." To which she replies, "If I had more time, I'd sit in a waiting room doing absolutely nothing." (Cue blank stares.)

My friend's point is, you *do* have the time to pursue your goals. You just need to be creative about finding and using that time. Even if you work 80 hours per week (is anyone ever really *working* all those hours?) and have six kids at home, you have spare minutes during the day. Vow to use every one of them to Commit to your goal.

The few minutes when you're waking up before your feet hit the floor in the morning. Your lunch break. Your toddler's naptime. Your commute time. The time between when your kids go to bed and you hit the sack. The minutes spent waiting in the dentist's office. Your life is filled with spare time. It doesn't *feel* significant because it's scattered in small chunks throughout the day, but you can leverage those minutes and make them work for you.

This is a great one to combine with other Commit tactics. For example, if you want to learn French, you can listen to language learning CDs in the car and while you're on the tread-mill at the gym; hire a French tutor to come to your office during your lunch break; surf French language websites instead of Facebook; or use an app like Duolingo when you're on the toilet. (Why not?)

If your goal is to get in shape, pump out push-ups between tasks at work; do crunches on your mattress before you get out of bed; hit the gym with your spouse on date night; do a quick stretching routine in the shower; perform calf raises while in line at the supermarket; *run* with your toddler on the play-ground instead of watching her from a bench.

Commit NOW! Be creative: How can you fit your Commit methods into the spare moments of your day? Write down your ideas and resolve to start today. In fact, if you have time to read this book right now, do you have time to make progress toward your goal before you read on?

COMMIT TACTIC #13: DELIBERATELY MOVE FASTER.

*W*hen you wash the dishes, can you will your hands to move faster than your usual speed so you get them done more quickly? Yes, you probably can. Can you take a quicker shower if you will yourself to? I'd say yes. Can you challenge yourself to type faster? Most likely.

Many people think the natural speed they happen to work at is the best they can do. But, believe it or not, you can make a deliberate decision to move faster when you do anything, including solving a problem or going after your goals.

Many guru-types out there sing the praises of slowing down, but "slow" isn't always the best strategy when you're trying to bust out of a rut. Here are some examples of how moving faster can work as a Commit tactic:

- If enhanced work productivity is your goal (maybe because you're after a promotion), focus on whipping through your emails so you have time for more important work matters.
- Time yourself as you write a report, pack a box, record an expense, send an invoice, or stuff an

envelope. When you next have to do this task, try to cut your time in half.

- If you want to become a fitness competitor, can you hurry up and hire a trainer today...call the gym right now...and move as quickly as you can to find and buy ten fitness-related books?
- Kids' bedtime ritual driving you crazy? ("Dad, can you get me a glass of water?" "Mom, will you read me one more story?") See if you can shorten the time it takes to get them into bed by half.
- Want to lose weight? If you normally stroll on the treadmill, pick up the pace a little. (Keeping safety in mind first, of course!)
- If your goal is to declutter your home, concentrate on making faster decisions on whether to save, toss, or donate old items. Get three boxes and chuck, chuck, chuck.

Commit NOW! Determine the next step toward your goal, pinpoint a task you're already doing, or choose one of the *Commit NOW!* assignments in this book—and resolve to do it at double speed.

COMMIT TACTIC #14: SURF YOUR WAY TO SUCCESS.

*J*f you're like most people, you're already spending a lot of time aimlessly surfing the internet. Why not turn that idle browsing into a Commit tactic that will give you the know-how and motivation to make strides toward your goal?

Whatever your problem or goal, there are bound to be dozens, if not hundreds, of blogs, videos, podcasts, and websites devoted to it, created by people who are passionate about the topic. Not all websites, videos, and podcasts are worth your time —but if you notice that one has a lot of followers or garners tons of social media shares, that usually means it contains information others find useful. You probably will, too.

It worked for me: I once decided to cut down on my work schedule to homeschool our son. But could we afford for me to chop my income in half? Would we go broke and end up living in our car?

On top of hiring an accountant and a financial advisor to help figure out the money situation (hiring people is a tactic we talk about later, and has been *well* worth the expense every time I've used it), I scoured the internet and added a bunch of money-saving, stay-at-home-mom, and budgeting blogs to my reading list.

Using the advice I read on these blogs, I managed to cut our food bill in half. In half! I decreased other expenses as well; for example, one blog mentioned that most of us are paying for too much data on our cellphone plans, so I visited AT&T and saved $40 per month by choosing a plan with less (but still more than enough) data based on our usage. Decreasing the data plan on my iPad saved an additional $30 per month. Another blog talked about how to save on insurance, and I cut our home and auto insurance costs by $700 per year following their simple advice.

Commit NOW! Right this instant, search for and bookmark (or subscribe to) 20 websites, podcasts, or video channels that are relevant to your goal or problem. Then schedule reading/listening/viewing time in your calendar.

COMMIT TACTIC #15: MEASURE EVERYTHING.

I'll never forget the story I read about an engineer who lost weight by doing nothing but tracking his weight daily and plotting it on a graph. No dieting, no exercise. Why did it work? Who knows...maybe the engineer began subconsciously cutting calories because he was made aware of his weight and his goals every single day.

But however it works, there's something powerful and inspiring about measuring your progress toward your goals. Seeing your progress in written form is pretty exciting, and learning how you tick can be enlightening—and motivating. Oh, so *that's* how much I eat! *That's* how much I've been saving toward my dream trip! *That's* how many words of Spanish I now know!

You can measure your progress in pen in a notebook; using apps that measure your steps, spending, and so on; or by creating fancy full-color spreadsheets, charts, and graphs that you hang on your wall.

This tactic works for so many goals it's not even funny. For example, you can track:

- Calories consumed
- Words written
- Minutes practicing your music
- Weight lifted
- Weight lost
- Money saved
- Money earned
- Number of times you say "I love you" to your kids
- Percent of your dissertation completed
- Sales letters mailed
- Days in a row you got up early
- Deals sealed
- Total minutes you meditated daily

I could go on, but you get the idea. Keep in mind that this practice is helpful even if your numbers start going the wrong way; when this happens, you can nip the problem in the bud before it turns into a free-fall. Broke the chain of getting up early? Resolve not to let one late morning turn into two. Weight loss plateauing? Try another Commit tactic, like hiring a pro to help you mix up your workout routine.

Commit NOW! Write down which aspects of your goal are measurable, and how you plan to track them. Will you keep a daily journal of your numbers, create a chart, use an app, or even post your results on Facebook? Then, starting today: Do it.

5

NOUN POWER

*R*emember learning in elementary school that nouns are "people, places, and things"? In this chapter I'll be revealing details about how to leverage the power of people, places, and things as a way to Commit. You'll learn why you should get the gear you need, how to crowdsource your Commit practice, why it's important to dedicate a special space for your practice, and more.

COMMIT TACTIC #16: HIRE HELP.

*W*hen I realized I was having trouble getting down onto and up from the floor when I played with my preschooler and was experiencing some hip pain during the day, I hired a private yoga instructor once a week to take me through yoga routines that would improve my hip strength and flexibility. A few months later, I was able to leap up off the floor instead of hobbling to my feet like an old lady—and I was able to move on to improving other aspects of my health with my instructor as well.

(For many people, their idea of solving the problem would be to not sit on the floor anymore, or to pop an Advil before playing with their kid. That's the *opposite* of Committing!)

Hiring someone to help you is truly Committing. You're telling yourself the problem or goal is important enough to spend money on, and important enough for other people to be working on as well. Nothing gets you fired up like knowing (1) you spent money getting someone to help you, (2) someone's got your back, and (3) that person is waiting for you right now.

You don't need to go into debt to hire a pro, but if you can reasonably afford to get someone to help you as one of your many Commit tactics, I strongly recommend it.

Here are some ideas for hiring people as a way to Commit:

- If you're looking to improve your business, hire a business coach. Having someone you already paid waiting for you to call and discuss your business puts it front and center in your life.
- If your big problem is that you're procrastinating on creating your website, hire a website designer to create the layout and graphics, and a copywriter to write the text. These people will expect you to come through with the info they need to get the job done, so your website is guaranteed to be completed quickly (and well!).
- Want to become a professional photographer? Hire a local pro to show you the ropes.
- If getting a handle on your finances is your goal, hire a financial advisor and an accountant. I did this and we ended up wiping out *all* our debt in one fell swoop.
- To Commit to fighting a lifestyle-related disease, hire a personal trainer and a nutritionist.
- If your relationship with your kids is in big trouble, start visiting a family therapist.
- You're an aspiring self-published author? Hire pros to create a cover design, edit and proofread your book, format the interior, and market your masterpiece. Hiring all these people ahead of time means the book will get done.

Again, this is not cheap—but Committing is about throwing massive resources at a problem or goal, including money.

If you really, really can't spare the cash, brainstorm ways you can make this tactic work without any monetary outlay. For example, if you want to switch careers, find a mentor in your chosen career through an industry organization. If you're an artist looking to get healthy, work out a trade with a personal trainer—you design her marketing materials, and she trains you.

Commit NOW! Find an expert you can hire: Ask friends, request recommendations on social media, and search Google and LinkedIn to find just the right professional. As soon as you can, reach out to a few pros via email or phone to request information or set up an exploratory meeting.

COMMIT TACTIC #17: CROWDSOURCE IT.

*P*icture hundreds, or even thousands, of people banding together to help you reach your most cherished goal or solve your most pressing problem. They cheer you on, give you advice, and even help fund your dream.

Crowdsourcing is leveraging the power of many people to get something done. For example, you might be familiar with the crowdfunding site Kickstarter, where entrepreneurs ask the public to help them fund their idea by pre-ordering their product in exchange for incentives.

Crowdsourcing is getting accountability and ideas, times a thousand. You can tap the brainpower of the multitudes to help you Commit to your goal in a massive way. For example:

- Some authors crowdsource their books: They simply open up a Google Drive file for the book and let their readers loose in there to add comments, make edits, and provide feedback.
- Maybe your goal is to go green and help save the planet. If you have a lot of friends on Facebook, post a

message asking everyone for their best tips on
greening up your home.

- Kickstart your board game, new gadget, or cool shoe
  design. If you're successful, hundreds of new
  customers will be giving you feedback and
  accountability, not to mention funding.
- If you want to become a better human and grow as a
  person, email all your friends, relatives, and even
  exes to ask for their honest feedback on the three
  areas where you can use improvement.

Just about any problem or goal lends itself to crowdsourcing
if you get creative about it. Putting yourself out there to the
masses also provides accountability; you wouldn't want to ask
500 people for ideas on going green and then not follow up with
what you've accomplished.

Commit NOW! In your Commit notebook, write down how you
plan to crowdsource ideas, accountability, and help for your
project or problem. Can you tap your Facebook friends, your
Twitter followers, your email address book, an online forum full
of industry colleagues, a crowdfunding site, or the throngs of
people on the sidewalk downtown? Then: Do it right now.

COMMIT TACTIC #18: GEAR UP.

*Y*ou'd love to learn Japanese in preparation for a dream trip, but you balk at the idea of spending hundreds on a set of language learning CDs, or even spending a few bucks on an app that can help. So you borrow a Japanese textbook from the library, flip through it halfheartedly, and give up. Or maybe you want to cook like a pro, but become discouraged when you try to sauté vegetables for your ratatouille in an old non-stick pan that doesn't live up to its name. Sound familiar?

One common problem when it comes to Committing is that we set goals we're passionate about, and then don't have the resources we need to truly go after them. We don't want to spend money, so we settle for going without—when having the right equipment would help us reach our goals much more quickly, efficiently, and pleasantly.

Whatever your goal is, investing in the equipment you'll need to make it happen is how you truly Commit. For example:

- To become a pro golfer, you could limp along with

your old, cheap equipment...or you could buy high-quality golfing equipment.

- If you're looking for a new job, invest in a sharp new interviewing suit, a copywriter to improve your LinkedIn profile, a career coach who can help you brush up on your interviewing skills, and a laptop videocam for video interviews.

- When you're launching a new business, instead of dealing with an ancient computer and scrambling every time you need a paper clip, buy a new laptop, the appropriate software, and all the office supplies you might need.

- Looking to add more spirituality to your life? Depending on your exact goals, you might want to treat yourself to a meditation cushion, a beautiful journal and quality pen, incense, a yoga mat, or religious texts.

Note: The purpose of this Commit tactic is *not* to guilt you into Committing: "I just spent $1,800 on this new MacBook, so now I'll really need to start my business or I'll feel like a jerk." No! The purpose is to arm you with everything you'll need to Commit to your goal with ease.

Spending the time and money to acquire the right supplies and equipment tells your mind that you're serious about your goal. Whenever I use this Commit tactic, I'm rewarded with a sense of certainty, clarity, and confidence: I know what I need to do, *and I have what I need to do it.*

Commit NOW! List in your Commit journal the equipment and supplies that will help you more easily reach your goal or solve your problem. Then, right now if you can, go online and order those items or schedule a time in your calendar to head out on a shopping expedition. Short on cash? Try bartering for the products you want, or ask for these items as gifts for your birthday or the winter holidays. It won't have the same effect as buying it all at once, but you gotta do what you gotta do!

COMMIT TACTIC #19: MAKE SPACE.

You're launching a retail website—from your kitchen, in view of teetering piles of dirty dishes. Or you're Committing to becoming more spiritual, and the only place you have to meditate and journal is in the living room, where your spouse has the TV blaring and the kids are tearing around like caffeinated monkeys.

Do you see how you're compromising your Commit practice when you have to *make do*? Committing is about figuring out the *best* way to reach your goals, not settling for just okay.

If you're going after a big goal or tackling a big problem, it's worth having a space that's dedicated to your Commit practice —one that's all decked out with the gear we talked about in the last Commit tactic. Having your own space is highly motivating, and will also help you reach your goals more easily.

As with all Commit tactics, you may need to use your creativity to come up with a solution. For your spirituality Commit, try turning a corner of your bedroom into a meditation area. If you're starting a business, well, how often do you really use that guest room—and what's more important to you right now, the twice-yearly guest or the future of your career?

You can also combine your need for a dedicated space with the Commit tactic "Go big or go home." When I was Committing to my freelance writing business years back and didn't have space in my home, I worked in a rent-by-the-hour office when I had a complicated project I needed to concentrate on. Eventually, I started renting an office space downtown for $400 per month. I figured if having a dedicated office helped me land an extra $400 assignment per month, it was worth the money.

Here are some ideas for spaces you can set up that will help you Commit:

- An unused home office in a friend's house.
- A rent-by-the-hour office space.
- A co-working space where you pay a monthly fee for unlimited access.
- A corner of a quiet room in your house, separated from the rest of the room with a folding screen.
- Your car. Yes, it is possible to turn your car into a workspace for those times when you're waiting to pick up your kid at the dance studio or when you arrive early at an appointment.
- A basement or garage gym.
- Rented office space outside the home.
- A garage studio for your art or craft.
- A backyard shed converted into a writing studio.
- A desk in your guest room. (Believe me, guests will not care that there is a computer desk in the room they sleep in once a year.)

If possible, make your space *your space*. By that I mean you stock it with all the right equipment and supplies; create a vision board you can gaze at between tasks; and decorate in such a way that you'll enjoy spending time there.

Commit *NOW!* In your Commit journal, brainstorm ideas for spaces to devote to your Commit practice. The earlier Commit tactic to come up with 100 ideas can work here. Today, do whatever is required to get the ball rolling: Call the friend who has an unused room in her home, check Craigslist for rentals, shop for a folding screen, or look into plans for building that backyard shed.

COMMIT TACTIC #20: LET THE COMPETITION SPUR YOU ON.

*S*omeone else could be turning *your* brilliant idea into a bestselling novel. Another person is starting the same business as you. There's a runner out there who works harder than you do. In short, someone else is Committing to *your* goal.

Here's a quote that really reflects the Commit attitude:

"Competing in sports has taught me that if I'm not willing to give 120 percent, somebody else will." —Ronald Blomberg (former Major League Baseball player)

Use your natural sense of competitiveness to Commit to fulfilling your goal or knocking out your problem with motivation and passion. For example:

- Create a workplace competition to see who can lose the most weight in three months.
- If you want to write a memoir, combine this Commit tactic with the earlier one to read ten books: Read ten bestselling memoirs and Commit to making yours a hundred times better than those.

- Got your eye on that smart, good-looking, talented man or woman? Yeah, so does everyone else. What can *you* do right now to tilt the odds in your favor, instead of just pining away?
- If you're raising money for a non-profit organization, find out who the number one individual fundraiser is and vow to beat their numbers. (It's for a good cause, right?)
- Research your five biggest business competitors to figure out what they're doing better than you, and resolve to move heaven and earth to top them.

Don't stand by and watch someone else Commit to a goal *you* want to achieve.

Commit NOW! Whatever your goal is, find out who's doing it best—then resolve to do even better.

6

PUTTING IT ALL TOGETHER

*a*re you feeling all pumped up? Are you ready to stop inching toward your goals and instead propel yourself past all obstacles until you get what you really want? Great!

Here's where we take all the strategies you've learned so far and figure out how to make them work together, plus how to overcome the common roadblock of not being *ready* to Commit.

COMBINE TO COMMIT.

*T*o Commit to solving a problem or reaching a goal, one option is to choose just one unbelievably big action, as we discussed above. However, relying on only one tactic sometimes backfires. For example, many people plan to get in shape by purchasing an expensive gym membership. "I'm paying a hundred bucks per month, so I'll *have* to go!" they say. We all know how that ends up.

Since the motivating factor of Committing is the initial, massive explosion of action that propels you forward, it's often more effective to combine two or more tactics.

So if you want to improve your physique, don't just throw money into a gym membership and call it a day. Join the gym *and* hire a trainer *and* make a pledge on Facebook *and* read 10 books on weight loss and muscle building *and* get a running partner who's waiting for you at 5 am every day.

If you're all about getting your commercial cleaning business off the ground, read ten books on running a business *and* hire a business coach *and* call 50 prospects a day *and* bookmark the 20 blogs and podcasts devoted to entrepreneurship *and* get up at early every day to work on developing a killer website.

Whatever you can think of that will demolish your problem or push you to your goal—do it *all at once*.

Take the woman I know who set the goal to complete ten unassisted chin-ups in a row, starting from zero and with no weight training experience. She combined three Commit tactics:

1. She hired a personal trainer.
2. She read everything she could on how to improve chin-up numbers.
3. She tracked every number she could think of related to her goal. In doing so, she noticed that she plateaued on the odd numbers, so she created a workout customized to help her perform more chin-ups.

On November 13, 2014, she reached her goal. "The last few were incredibly hard, and not super-pretty, but I did it. (And my trainer has the video to prove it)," she writes. "After the eighth one, I knew that I was going to get there that day. I think I smiled for a week."

That's what I call combining to Commit. This woman threw so many tactics at the goal that failure was simply not an option.

Doesn't combining Commit tactics take a lot of effort? Yes. But the trick is, if you put forth an immense amount of effort up front—one initial massive push—the ball will start rolling, and it will *keep* rolling with a lot less work.

COMMIT FIRST, WORK OUT THE DETAILS LATER.

*T*oo many goal-setters get derailed when they try to Commit because they don't have all their ducks in a row. "I can't start *now*," they moan. "First I need to do X, Y, and Z, and I really don't know how to do those things." This is called *perfectionism*, and it's nothing but a stalling tactic.

Commit first, *then* worry about the details. For example, when I'm starting on a new book, I often get the cover designed right away and put out the word that the book will be released on X date. On my last two books (including this one), I posted the three covers I had had designed and asked readers to pick their favorite—before I had even written the books.

This is called the ready...fire...aim approach. You get into your ready stance, take the action, examine the results, and then re-aim if necessary and try again. It reminds me of another of my favorite quotes: "*Completion trumps perfection.*"

Here are some ways to jump into Committing before you're "ready":

- If you're planning to hire people to help you reach your goal, round them up and get the contracts signed before you even get to work, or before you have a schedule or a plan worked out. For example, if you're hiring a personal trainer, sign up for a package of ten sessions and *then* worry about making the sessions fit your schedule. If you want to start a business, sign a contract with a business coach before you do anything else.

- If putting some skin in the game is one of your strategies, promise a deliverable to a whole bunch of people by X date—*then* figure out how to produce it by the deadline.

- Pick three random weekdays—*any* days—and ask a friend to go running on those mornings to help you prepare for that 5k. Instead of dithering about how to fit running into your schedule and putting it off until the perfect opportunity presents itself (which will never happen), you now have to make it work. "Monday, Wednesday, and Friday before work, great, let's do this. Oops, it's my turn to get the kids ready for school on Mondays...better revise the schedule with my spouse. And I just remembered I hate getting up early...I need to figure out how I can get to bed earlier so I'm not wiped out in the morning."

- A personal example: When I decided to become a personal trainer several years ago, I rented a studio and stocked it with hundreds of dollars worth of equipment before I even had my first client, and spread the word that I was offering a free training session to 50 people—before I even knew how to create an effective workout. Knowing I was all set with the equipment I needed, and that a bunch of people were expecting free sessions from me, motivated me to put the rest of the details in place.

LIMIT YOUR COMMIT PRACTICE.

*a*t this point, you may be feeling a little overwhelmed with the idea of Committing. It is a lot to think about and do.

Try to remember that this massive push is temporary. You're pushing just long enough to set things in motion and automate your progress. For example, if your goal is to become a freelance writer, you'll want to pump out an incredible number of pitches to get traction. But eventually, you'll have a stable of regular writing clients and won't need to toil away at pitching so much. As another example, when you Commit to losing weight, eventually you'll reach your goal weight and will go into maintenance mode.

If it helps, set a limit for how long you'll adhere to your Commit plan. You might resolve to go all-in for only a week, two weeks, two months, or however long you estimate it will take to see results.

Can you imagine filling every spare moment of your day in pursuit of your goal, or having to pay for help, or reading massive numbers of books—forever? Luckily, it's not necessary.

Keep that in mind when you're feeling overwhelmed with the idea of Committing.

7

TROUBLESHOOTING

Committing can be scary. You're putting a lot on the line! So I've got some thoughts to help get you past the most common roadblocks.

COMMIT ROADBLOCK #1: "I DON'T HAVE THE TIME TO COMMIT TO A GOAL THAT WAY."

*O*ne of my favorite time management books is *168 Hours: You Have More Time Than You Think* by Laura Vanderkam. The message is that there are 168 hours in a week, and even if you work 40 hours per week and sleep eight hours a night, that leaves 72 hours per week free and clear.

Please don't tell me that your housework, childcare duties, and volunteer commitments take up 72 hours a week! Somewhere in there is the time to write out a list of 100 ideas, read through ten books, round up hired help, and devise an accountability system for yourself.

Also, don't forget that Committing is sometimes about making hard choices. Maybe to reach your goals, in the short term you'll have to stop watching TV, cut down on your Facebook time, or say no to some commitments that you didn't really want to do anyway. You may have to shuffle your daily tasks and to-dos around so you have a solid block of time for your Commit practice. Or you might even decide to adopt a different sleep schedule from the rest of your family so you can Commit after everyone goes to bed or before they wake up. (I find that 6 am—

an hour and a half before my usual wake-up time—is the perfect time to work on my business goals.)

COMMIT ROADBLOCK #2: "I JUST DON'T FEEL MOTIVATED TO EVEN START."

A very smart lady I once interviewed for an article told me, "You don't act because you feel motivated...you feel motivated because you act." That's right—motivation follows *after you start working on something.*

Ever notice how sometimes you can't motivate yourself to remove your butt from the sofa and get the housework done? But if by some chance you did get up and start working, you'd find yourself on a roll and suddenly you're cleaning the whole house and scrubbing the baseboards to boot? That's because taking action got you all fired up. That's how it works.

If you have a problem to solve or a dream to reach for, don't wait until you feel divinely inspired, because it won't happen. Instead, take the very first action step, and after a few minutes you probably won't want to stop.

For example, if you take the initial step of emailing a nutritionist, she'll call you up. Then it follows naturally that you'll talk about her program...and by this point you're probably feeling pretty motivated. Then you'll sign on for a few sessions. Then she'll be waiting for you in her office at an appointed time and your Commit plan is set in motion with that one tiny step.

So if you're not feeling motivated, that's okay. You're not supposed to feel motivated. You're supposed to take action. *Then* you'll feel motivated.

COMMIT ROADBLOCK #3: "I WANT TO DO IT ALL PERFECTLY, WHICH IS IMPOSSIBLE...SO I NEVER START COMMITTING."

One of my favorite quotes comes from General George S. Patton:

"A good solution applied with vigor now is better than a perfect solution applied ten minutes later."

With Committing, the idea is to move fast. You don't have time to make it perfect. You'll work out the details as you go along. The important thing is to take massive action right away.

I used to mentor writers, and you wouldn't believe what perfectionists they are! I always told them that a great article pitch you send out now has an infinitely better chance at being accepted than the one you never send out because you're busy trying to "perfect" it. The same goes with Committing. Get it done and get it done fast, and worry about the details later. Action always trumps perfection.

You know the saying "Good enough never is"? I call B.S. My own saying is "Good enough usually is."

COMMIT ROADBLOCK #4: "I DON'T HAVE THE MONEY TO COMMIT."

*S*ome of the suggestions I've given in this book do require an outlay of cash. But as I keep saying, you don't necessarily have to spend a lot of—or even *any*—money to Commit.

Accountability buddies cost zilch. Libraries are free. You may be able to find a mentor gratis through an industry organization. Blogs, podcasts, and instructional videos are likewise free. A workout or running partner you find through one of the many websites out there for this purpose shouldn't be charging you. Posting a pledge on Facebook? You got it: Free.

That said, the same thing I said about time applies to money: You probably have some, but it's more comfortable to keep spending it on nice-to-haves like restaurant meals, cable TV, or your extensive collection of video games.

It's the change that's scary, not the fact that you're spending money. You're already spending money. You just need to change what you're spending it on. Saying no to buying something so you can say yes to your goals: That's Committing.

8

WHAT IF YOU'RE REALLY, REALLY NOT
READY TO COMMIT?

*S*ometimes Committing just won't work, and the reason may be that your goal isn't right for you. You're pushing to reach a goal you don't truly want, and part of you knows that.

Believe me, I know from experience. I've always wanted to be a hardcore athlete, running marathons, pumping iron, and sweating it out in martial arts classes. I even dreamed of becoming a fitness competitor—you know, one of those athletes with like 6% body fat.

I tried Committing in so many ways, but would quickly lapse back into my old habits once I eased off on my Commit tactics. I wanted to *love* exercise, but it never happened. It was more like I was *tolerating* it.

Finally, I had the realization that while I enjoy reading about, writing about, and teaching fitness, I'm naturally more of a gentle exerciser. Whereas I had to force myself to do 5k training podcasts and weight training workouts *sans* trainer, I'm drawn to yoga and walking. My true purpose is not to have washboard abs, but to be healthy and energetic to keep up with my young son.

I don't even need to Commit to walk and take yoga classes: I seek out opportunities to do these things as much as I can. While the idea of becoming an elite athlete is attractive—I mean, who wouldn't want to look like an Olympian and be able to perform superhero feats of strength if they could wave a wand and make it so?—it's just not me. The whole time, I thought what I wanted was to be a hardcore athlete, and that's what I tried Committing to. But it was the wrong goal all along.

So that's why Committing may not work for you in every situation. If you're having a hard time staying motivated or reaching your goals even though you're Committing the heck out of them, examine whether you really want these goals—or just think you *should* want them, or whether your real goal is something just slightly different (as mine was).

I don't want to be one of those authors who blames the reader: "If my plan doesn't work for you, it's because you don't want it badly enough...loser." But it is a possibility, as I learned from personal experience, that your goals aren't truly resonating with you.

It's okay to drop a goal, even a long-held one. This is all a learning process, and with experience you'll figure out what's right for *you*.

9

FINAL THOUGHTS

I want you to succeed, and I know you can do it...because I've Committed my way to success many times. Committing has helped me beat panic and depression, get healthy, build a thriving business, save money, and more. The Commit philosophy keeps me highly motivated and active.

The more you can throw at a problem or goal right off, the easier it will be to wrestle it into submission. To extend the wrestling metaphor, Committing is like going into a wrestling match against an one opponent with ten guys on your side.

You win!

Let's Help Others, Too!

If this book has helped you, I urge you to pass it along to others. Let your friends and family members borrow your copy, or even better, buy them their very own copy for their birthday or Christmas. Or, heck, buy the book for them as a gift *just because*. What better way to tell someone you love them than to help them reach all their dreams?

Also, I hope you'll take a few minutes to review *Commit* on

Amazon.com, Goodreads, or wherever you review books—and be sure to share your own tips to help others get the most out of this book.

Thank you so much for reading this book. I hope it helps you reach your most important goals and solve your most pressing problems.

ABOUT THE AUTHOR

Linda Formichelli left a boring office job, where she spent hours each day playing Minesweeper, to become a full-time freelance writer in 1997. Since then, she's written for over 150 magazines—including *Redbook, Writer's Digest, Health,* and *Parenting*—and more than two dozen copywriting and content clients like CVS, TripAdvisor, and OnStar.

She's also the co-publisher at Renegade Writer Press, which offers books for writers and other smart people, like these beauties:

- *How to Do It All: The Revolutionary Plan to Create a Full, Meaningful Life — While Only Occasionally Wanting to Poke Your Eyes out with a Sharpie,* by Linda Formichelli
- *Money Shots: How to Save Cash on Your Coffee Habit — While Still Feeling Full & Satisfied,* by Linda Formichelli & Diana Burrell
- *The Renegade Writer: A Totally Unconventional Guide to Freelance Writing Success,* by Linda Formichelli & Diana Burrell
- *From Pitch to Published: How to Sell Your Article Ideas to Magazines,* by Linda Formichelli & Diana Burrell
- *Get the Gig: 10 Secrets to Writing Better Story Pitches for Magazines,* by Diana Burrell
- *Getting In,* an erotic novel by Isabella Jones

- *The Happiest Ending*, an erotic short by Frida Wildman

Visit the Renegade Writer Press site (www.renegadewriterpress.com) to check out (and purchase!) books for writers, self-help books, erotic novels, and books on food & home—and to get the scoop on upcoming books. (Don't worry, you can choose which genres we'll send you info on. :)

Again, thanks for reading *Commit*. Now...let's get out there and make things happen!

ACKNOWLEDGMENTS

I have so many people to thank for their support as I was writing *Commit!* I'm deeply grateful to have so many great friends, family members, and readers.

My husband Eric, son Traver, and exchange student Pegah put up with me as I obsessed about *Commit* for months on end. Eric also edited my manuscript and helped brainstorm ideas for getting the word out about this book. Thank you!

Thanks to my mom and dad, who watched Traver while I was editing *Commit*.

Thanks also to my friend and *Renegade Writer Press* co-publisher Diana Burrell for looking over my manuscript—twice! Her comments, anecdotes, and edits made this book sharper and more powerful, not to mention she laid out the interior of this book.

Daisha Cassell offered some helpful comments and spotted several typos that had slipped through the almost-final draft. You rule!

I appreciate that Dianna Gunn and Kirsetin Morello shared their stories of how they used Commit tactics to improve their lives. Thank you!